WHO IS GOD?
FROM A TO Z

WRITTEN BY:
KIMBERLY J. MAXWELL

ILLUSTRATED BY:
KELLY D. JOHNSON

ISBN: 979-8-218-27538-9

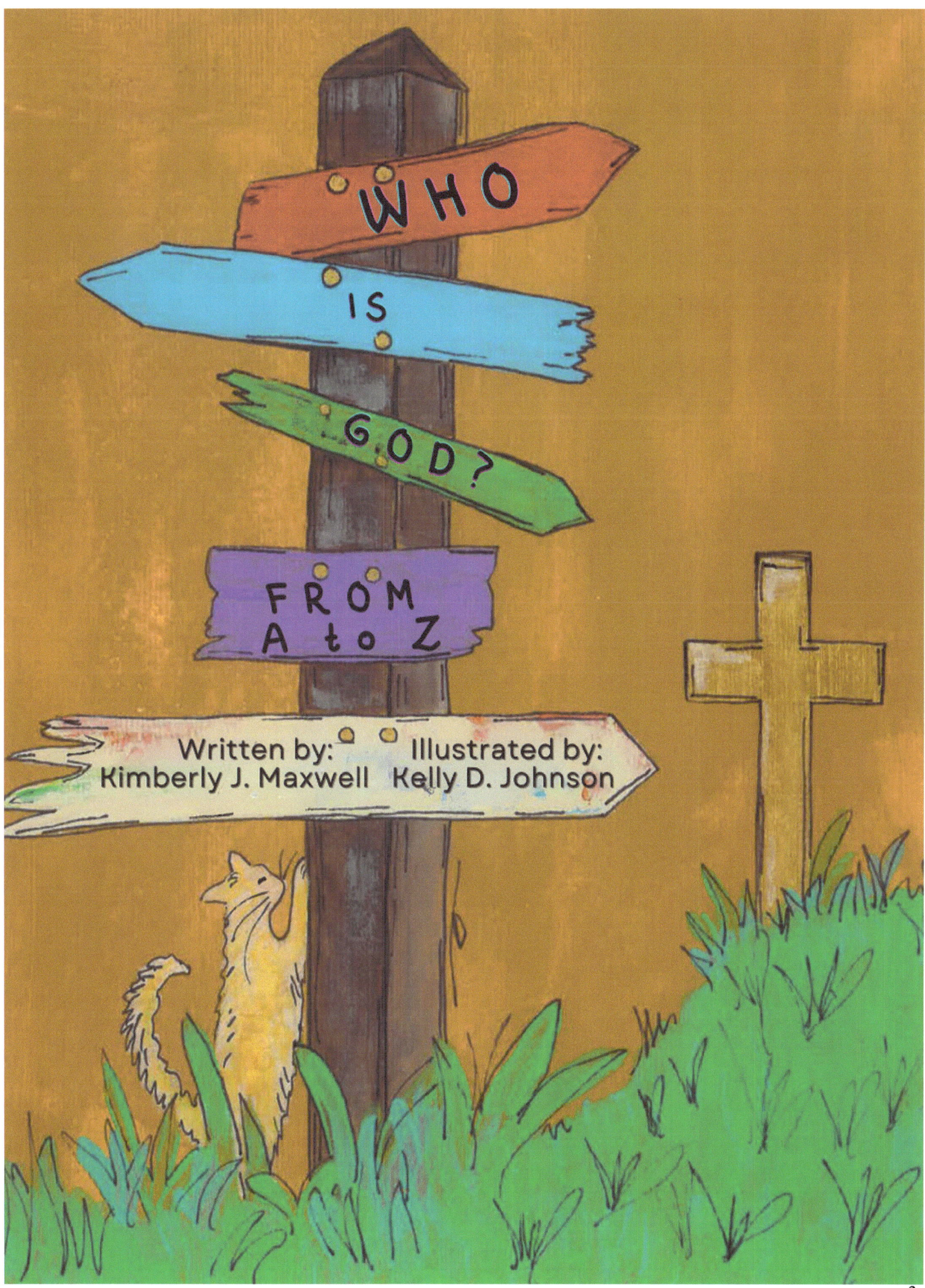

WHO
IS
GOD?
FROM
A to Z
Written by: Illustrated by:
Kimberly J. Maxwell   Kelly D. Johnson

I dedicate this book:

To God
the author and perfecter of my faith.

To Steve
the love of my life, my inspiration, and my encourager.

To Nathan and Brynna
our extravagant gifts from God. You have brought us so much joy!

AND

To Astro
our favorite cat. Can you spot him on each page?

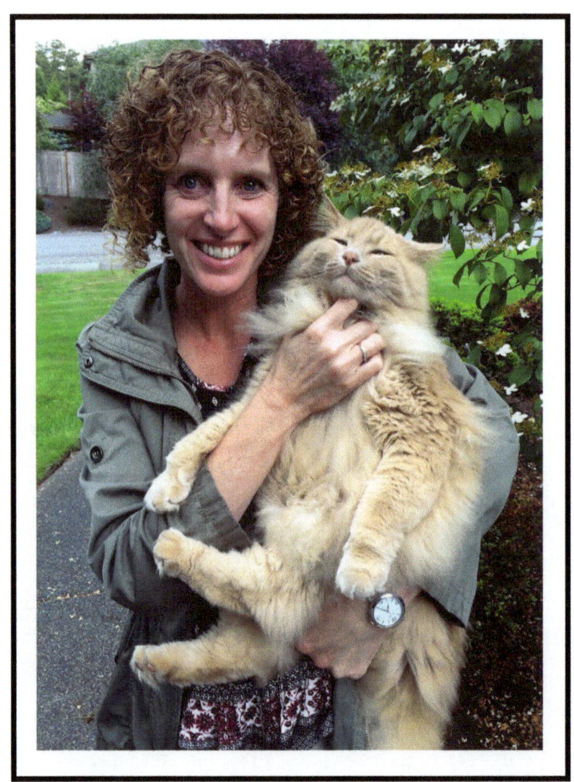

And what is eternal life? It is knowing You, the only true God, and Jesus Christ, whom You have sent. – John 17:3

A note to parents and grandparents:

In my elementary school years, most Sundays my sister and I walked to a little neighborhood church just a few blocks from our house. I went to Sunday School, sang in the children's choir, and sat in "Big Church" with my friend and her family.

One day, my Sunday School teacher shared Revelation 3:20 with me. She said Jesus was standing at the door of my heart knocking, and He wanted me to hear His voice and open the door so that He could come into my life and be with me forever. Perhaps she shared this verse out of its original context, but it impacted me, and that night, lying in bed, I opened my heart up to Jesus and invited Him in. I believed.

Sometime later, I realized I needed God to forgive me. Around 4th or 5th grade, I became very aware of the things in my life that were making Him sad: I was often mean to my sister, I lied, I cheated, I was jealous, unforgiving, unkind to friends, selfish, and disrespectful of my parents. I knew I needed God's forgiveness if I wanted to have a relationship with Him. When the pastor invited people to come forward for prayer, I walked up the aisle, knelt at the foot of the cross, and asked Jesus to clean out my heart and make me new.

Walking home from church that day, I felt free and light, like I could jump up into the air and float home. My heart was filled with a joy and peace I had never known. I didn't just believe in Jesus anymore, now I had EXPERIENCED Him for myself. His Holy Spirit came into my heart that day and filled me with His presence.

For over forty years now I have been learning more and more, with the Holy Spirit's help, how to recognize God's presence, hear His voice, and walk with Him in my everyday life. I long for this next generation (and the next and the next) to know and personally experience Him too, which is why I have written this book.

As you read it with the children in your life, pray that they will know and believe the truth about who Jesus is and love spending time with Him in His Word. Pray that they will increasingly understand and experience their heavenly Father's love for them (Ephesians 3:18-19). Pray that they will be continuously filled with the Holy Spirit so that they can live victoriously and joyfully as they work with Him to advance God's kingdom here on Earth. And no matter how old they are, continue praying for them. I have included some prayer cards at the end to help you get started (see page 61).

Enjoy reading this book as you get to know the God who knows us best and loves us most. What a privilege it is to disciple another generation of Jesus followers!

Contending in prayer with you for the next generation,

Kim

GOD IS THE ABSOLUTE TRUTH

"All your words are true. All your laws are right. They last forever."
– Psalm 119:160

"... it is impossible for God to lie." – Hebrews 6:18a (NLT)

SHARE: How do you know when something is true?

Absolute truth is everything in our world that is always true, no matter what. Take the law of gravity for example. What goes up must come down. Always. No matter what.

Just like gravity is always true, God is always true. Truth is who God is. God cannot lie. There is nothing false in Him.

Because all God's words are true, we can trust Him. People may say that they have "their" truth, and you have "your" truth, but Jesus said, "... I am ... <u>the</u> truth ..." (John 14:6a, emphasis added). Other people and religions may claim to have some truth, but their claims are not <u>the</u> truth.

Have you ever felt sad or scared about something that turned out great in the end? Our emotions are real and important, but they are often out of sync with the truth and don't always help us know what is true. Our emotions don't define truth. God does. That is why we must measure everything we see, hear, think, and feel with God's words so that we know what is true and what is not. It is so important to read our Bibles, so we know what God says and thinks and feels.

When we know the truth in God's Word, we are set free to become all that God wants us to be (John 8:32): filled with joy, purpose, love, peace, wisdom, strength, and goodness.

PRAYER: *God, You are the absolute truth. Please help me to love reading my Bible so that I can know You better and know what is true. Please set me free from anxiety, worry, fear, hatred, anger, guilt, and anything else that keeps me from being all You want me to be. Change my feelings and thoughts so that they are in sync with Your truth. And please show me how I can help others know You as the absolute truth.*

SHARE: Name some things that are always true, no matter what. (Example: 2 + 2 = 4)

GOD IS BEAUTIFUL

"I'm asking the LORD for only one thing. Here is what I want. I want to live in the house of the LORD all the days of my life. I want to look at the beauty of the LORD. I want to worship him in his temple." – Psalm 27:4

SHARE: What is the most beautiful thing you've ever seen?

God created everything beautifully –

> multicolored rainbows to remind us that He will always keep His promises,
> sparkling stars to remind us that He is the light in the darkness,
> fragrant flowers to remind us of His extravagant provision,
> fiery sunsets to remind us that He is always with us,
> snow-capped mountains to reflect His majesty,
> soaring eagles to point us to the freedom that is ours in Him, and
> roaring oceans to remind us of His power.

If all that He created is so wildly beautiful, just imagine what God must be like! His creation is just a tiny glimpse of His glory.

And if God is beautiful, you must be too, because you were created in His image (Genesis 1:27). You are God's magnificent masterpiece, created on purpose and for a purpose. You are His priceless work of art (Ephesians 2:10). He made your hair, your eyes, your skin. He decided how tall you will be, how smart and strong and fast you are. God has made you unique, different, and special. He knit you together with His very own hands just the way He meant you to be (Psalm 139: 13-14). He thinks you are <u>very</u> good (Genesis 1:31).

And He is still at work making you even more beautiful. People look at how someone appears on the outside, but God looks at what is in the heart (1 Samuel 16:7). He is placing people and circumstances in your life to teach you how to be kind, patient, compassionate, thoughtful, and trustworthy. He will use everything that happens in your life to make your heart more beautiful—more like Jesus (Romans 8:28-29). God chose you and carefully designed you to do good things that will spread His beauty around this world and help people come to know Him.

PRAYER: *God, help me see and experience Your beauty every day and worship You. Help me to care more about what people are like on the inside than what they look like on the outside. Remind me every day that I am Your beautiful masterpiece, created by You to do the good things You already have planned for me.*

SHARE: Where do you see God's beauty today?

GOD CARES

"Don't worry about anything; instead, pray about everything. Tell God what you need, and thank him for all he has done. Then you will experience God's peace, which exceeds anything we can understand. His peace will guard your hearts and minds as you live in Christ Jesus."
– Philippians 4:6-7 (NLT)

"Turn all your worries over to Him. He cares about you." – 1 Peter 5:7

SHARE: Who are some people who care for you?

God cares about you. He knows what time you go to bed and what time you get up (Psalm 121:8). He knows the number of hairs on your head (Luke 12:7)—even when the brush pulls some of them out.

God cares about you so much that He sent His only Son, Jesus, to take the punishment for your sin so that you can live forever with Him and be a part of His family (John 3:16).

God cares about what you have been through in the past and what you are going through now. God knows when you cry, and He cares for you when you are hurting (Psalm 56:8).

Everything God does, even the suffering He allows in your life is done out of love for you, and He is right there with you in the middle of it all. God understands, and He promises to work it all out for your good if you love Him—even the hard and sad things (Romans 8:28). God doesn't run from pain like people often do. He is not afraid of suffering or even death because He knows what is beyond this life—eternal joy for those who follow Him.

As a loving father, God will only give His children His very best for them, which is why He doesn't give you everything you ask for. Your trust in His love for you is more precious to God than pure gold (1 Peter 1:6-7). He will do whatever it takes to stretch it and grow it. So don't worry. Trust Him because He cares for you.

PRAYER: *God, help me to turn all my worries over to You and really believe that You care about me. Thank You for taking such good care of me. Thank You for sending Jesus to die for me. Help me to see others as You do and help me to care for them like You do.*

SHARE: What worry can you turn over to God? Open and hold out your hands. Imagine giving Him all your worries and receiving His peace and joy.

BIBLE
FAITH

GOD IS MY DEFENDER

"Don't be afraid of them. The LORD your God himself will fight for you."
– Deuteronomy 3:22

"…In all these things we are more than winners! We owe it all to Christ, who has loved us. I am absolutely sure that not even death or life can separate us from God's love. Not even angels or demons, the present or the future, or any powers can separate us. Not even the highest places or the lowest, or anything else in all creation can separate us. Nothing at all can ever separate us from God's love. That's because of what Christ Jesus our Lord has done." – Romans 8:37-39

SHARE: What does a soldier wear into battle?

Things happen in life that can knock us down and make us feel defeated, fearful, and discouraged. But we are never alone. The God of angel armies is in our battles with us. He never stops fighting with us and for us! He fights for:

> our belief and trust in Him,
> our joy,
> our peace,
> our hope,
> our victory over temptation and sin.

Yet God allows suffering and hardship in our lives. Why? To test and strengthen our faith and to make us strong and beautiful and more like Jesus. Though there will be times when the circumstances in your life may not be good, you can trust God because He is good, and He promises to be with you in every battle. You will never have to face anything without Him, and you can trust that there is purpose in everything He allows into your life.

Your relationship with God is more important to Him than anything else in this world (John 3:16). God will do whatever it takes to save you and defend you and help you become all that He has created you to be. He is more powerful than anyone or anything else in heaven or on earth. "What should we say then? Since God is on our side, who can be against us?" (Romans 8:31).

PRAYER: *Thank You, God, for defending me from the evil in this world. Help me to remember that You are a warrior, helping me fight my battles. Help me not to be afraid. Instead, help me to remember that You are always with me. And help me to trust that You are using everything in my life—the happy things and the hard things—to help me become more like Jesus.*

SHARE: What battle would you like God to help you fight today? (Examples: fear, anger, self-control)

GOD IS EXTRAVAGANT

"God is able to do far more than we could ever ask for or imagine. He does everything by his power that is working in us." – Ephesians 3:20

SHARE: If you could ask God for anything, what would it be?

One day, Jesus was at a wedding. Before the wedding was over, they ran out of wine. (In those days, clean drinking water was often not available, and wine represented life, joy, and blessing.) The family hosting the celebration would have been deeply embarrassed. But … Jesus was there.

"Six stone water jars stood nearby. The Jews used water from that kind of jar for special washings. They did that to make themselves pure and 'clean.' Each jar could hold 20 to 30 gallons.

Jesus said to the servants, 'Fill the jars with water.' So they filled them to the top.

Then he told them, 'Now dip some out. Take it to the person in charge of the dinner.'

They did what he said. The person in charge tasted the water that had been turned into wine. He didn't realize where it had come from. But the servants who had brought the water knew. Then the person in charge called the groom to one side. He said to him, 'Everyone brings out the best wine first. They bring out the cheaper wine after the guests have had too much to drink. But you have saved the best until now'" (John 2:6-10).

God loves to bless us with more than enough—above and beyond—extravagantly! Everything belongs to God (Psalm 50:10), and He loves to give us His very best. It brings Him great joy.

God loves to bless His children because He loves us so much. God ultimately displayed His extravagant love for us when "… He sent his one and only Son into the world. He sent him so we could receive life through him. Here is what love is. … It is that he loved us and sent his Son to give his life to pay for our sins" (1 John 4: 9-10).

PRAYER: *God, thank You for loving and blessing me extravagantly. Thank You for giving me Your very best — Your Son Jesus. Help me to give You the very best of my time, talents, and treasures. And help me to love and give to others extravagantly as well.*

SHARE: When has someone shown extravagant love to you? How can you express your love and gratitude to Jesus by giving generously, even extravagantly to someone else today?

WHEEL
bobby

GOD IS OUR FATHER

"This is how you should pray. 'Our Father in heaven, may your name be honored.'" – Matthew 6:9

"See what amazing love the Father has given us! Because of it, we are called children of God. And that's what we really are! The world doesn't know us because it didn't know him." – 1 John 3:1

SHARE: What is something you have asked one of your parents for recently? What did they say?

Do you know you have a Father in heaven?

When Jesus' disciples asked Him to teach them how to pray, Jesus told them to come to God in prayer like a child runs to his father: boldly, expectantly trusting Him to help (Hebrews 4:16).

Why? Because God is not only Jesus' Father. He is your Father too. God chose you to be His child before the world was even created (Ephesians 1:4). When you believe in His Son Jesus, you are adopted into God's family.

God is a good, strong, attentive, and loving father. He provides for and protects his children. He also perfectly teaches His children with compassion, kindness, wisdom, and gentleness. He can be trusted to do only what is best for His family.

Because you are God's deeply loved child, you get to inherit all the good things that He has for you:

His Holy Spirit,
His love,
His power,
His wisdom,
His forgiveness,
His peace,
His joy,
and best of all—eternal life with Him (Ephesians 1:7-21; Galatians 4:6-7).

PRAYER: *Thank You, God, for being a good and loving Father. Thank You for choosing me to be in Your family. Help me to come to you confidently when I pray, expectantly trusting You to do what is best for me.*

SHARE: What do you know about adoption? Do you know someone who has been adopted?

GOD IS GOOD

"I am sure that Your goodness and love will follow me all the days of my life…" – Psalm 23:6a

"I remain confident of this: I will see the goodness of the LORD in the land of the living. Wait for the LORD; be strong and take heart and wait for the LORD." – Psalm 27:13-14 (NIV)

"Taste and see that the LORD is good." – Psalm 34:8a

SHARE: What is your favorite dessert?

God is even better than ice cream! Too much ice cream can be bad for you, but God is completely, purely good. That means there is no bad or evil or injustice or hatred or unkindness or selfishness in Him. He can only do what is good. No one else is or has ever been completely good except God alone (Mark 10:18), and He longs to lavishly pour out His goodness on us (Isaiah 30:18). It brings Him glory and gives Him great pleasure to show His goodness to us.

Because He is good, God wants and knows what is best for us. Getting what we want when we want it is not always the best thing for us. Nor is it glorifying to God. When God doesn't give us what we've asked for, we can be sure that He has something even better planned. It may not look like we thought it would, but no matter what, we can be confident that God's plans are for our eternal good. "'My thoughts are not like your thoughts. And your ways are not like my ways,' announces the LORD. 'The heavens are higher than the earth. And my ways are higher than your ways. My thoughts are higher than your thoughts'" (Isaiah 55:8-9).

God has a greater purpose for us than our immediate comfort, and sometimes that means we must wait for God to show us how He is working all things for good in our lives (Romans 8:28).

Waiting is hard! But when we wait for the LORD, we can always have hope, because God has promised blessing and goodness for all who wait for Him (Isaiah 30:18).

PRAYER: *God, You are good. When You don't answer my prayers the way I want You to, help me to wait and trust You to work all things for my ultimate good and Your eternal glory (Romans 8:28). Help me to taste and see Your goodness today.*

SHARE: Where have you seen the goodness of God lately? Thank Him for it.

GOD HEARS

"After a long time, the king of Egypt died. The people of Israel groaned because they were slaves. They also cried out to God. Their cry for help went up to him. God heard their groans. He remembered his covenant with Abraham, Isaac and Jacob. So God looked on the Israelites with concern for them." – Exodus 2:23-25

"Never stop praying." – 1 Thessalonians 5:17

SHARE: What is something you have talked to God about recently?

God hears your prayers. He hears every word you speak. He hears your thoughts. He hears the groans of your hurting heart when you don't even know what to say (Romans 8:26-27). And God uses your prayers to accomplish His plans. By praying, we get to partner with Him as He rules this world.

He already knows everything, but He loves it when we invite Him into whatever we are doing, saying, thinking, or feeling. Not only does God hear you, He LOVES to hear you, and your prayers move Him to act.

You can talk to God anytime, anywhere, about anything. There is nothing too big or too small to talk to Him about. Ask Him:

> Which way should I go?
> What should I do next?
> Which is best?
> What does that mean?

Pour out your feelings, hurts, frustrations, fears, and joys to Him. Never stop praying (1 Thessalonians 5:17). Pray like you have a God in heaven who hears you … because you do. Then watch. Expect Him to answer. He will lead you and guide you in the way you should go (Psalm 32:8).

PRAYER: *God, thank You that You hear me. Remind me to share my thoughts and feelings and questions with You throughout my day. Help me to recognize Your voice when You speak to me, too. Help me to hear You and give me the courage to do what You say.*

SHARE: What would you like to talk to God about today? Take a few moments to talk to Him.

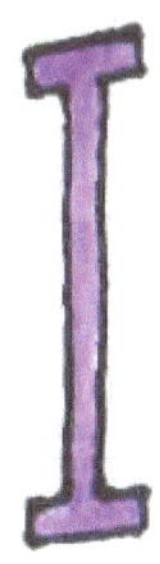

GOD IS INVISIBLE

"No one has ever seen God. But the One and Only is God and is at the Father's side. The one at the Father's side has shown us what God is like."
– John 1:18

SHARE: Look outside and see if the wind is blowing. How can you tell?

No one has ever seen the wind. But we have all seen evidence of the wind: leaves blowing, tree branches swaying, clouds moving, kites flying, boats sailing, windmills spinning. We have heard the wind whistle and slam doors. We have felt the wind cool us on a hot summer day and freeze our noses in the winter.

No one has ever seen God either, but you don't need to see Him to know that He is real. We have seen His power in a storm. We have heard His voice whisper to our hearts through His Word or a song. We have seen His beauty in a sunset. We have felt His care through someone's kindness. We have seen His love for us on the cross.

Even though we can't see God face to face yet, He is very real, and He wants us to know Him. God has left us His very own words in the Bible to show us what He is like. The more we soak in His words and live them out, the more we will look like Him, and others will see Him in us (John 15:4).

And someday soon, we <u>will</u> see Him face to face, and we will know Him fully, just like He knows us (1 Corinthians 13:12).

PRAYER: *God, we look forward to seeing You face to face one day. Until then, help us to recognize Your glory and Your power in the world around us. We want to see You and know You better. When other people look at us, may they see Your light, Your love, and Your life in everything we do and say.*

SHARE: Where have you seen evidence of God lately?

GOD IS JOYFUL

"… (The LORD) will sing for joy because of you." – Zephaniah 3:17e

"Always be joyful. Never stop praying. Give thanks no matter what happens. God wants you to thank him because you believe in Christ Jesus." – 1 Thessalonians 5:16-18

SHARE: What makes you happy?

God is deeply joyful! What fills God with joy? Everything that brings Him glory and honors His name: His beautiful creation, His Son Jesus, you, and me.

God sings for joy because of you! And because God is joyful, He wants us, His children, to be filled with joy too.

Happiness comes when the things around us are going well, but true joy does not depend on our outward circumstances. Joy is a goodness, a delight inside of us that only comes from God.

God IS our joy. Because of Him

>we have His peace,
>we have hope,
>we are forgiven,
>He walks with us,
>His Spirit is in us, and
>our future is secure with Him in heaven.

When we choose to trust God and His love for us and choose to praise Him and thank Him in every circumstance, we can be filled with joy even when we are sad (James 1:2). Praising God reminds us of who He is. Thanking God reminds us of what He has done. Both bring us great joy, and God is delighted when we enjoy Him.

So, no matter what happens today, we can choose to be joyful because of God. The joy of the LORD makes us strong (Nehemiah 8:10).

SHARE: What do you love about God? Spend some time enjoying Him together.

PRAYER: *God, I praise You for ____________________*

SHARE: What are you thankful for? Remember what God has done for you.

PRAYER: *God, I thank You for ____________________*

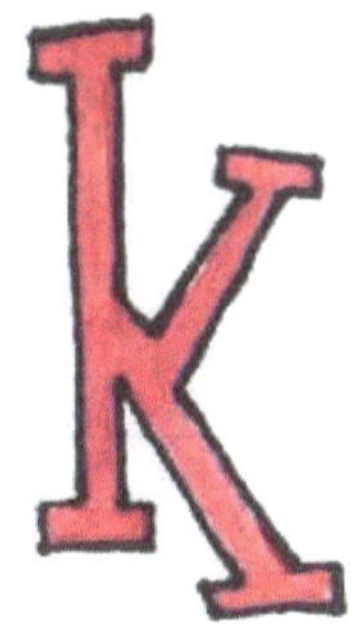

GOD IS KING

"… the LORD Most High is wonderful. He is the great King over the whole earth." – Psalm 47:2

"… God is the blessed and only Ruler. He is the greatest King of all. He is the most powerful Lord of all." – 1 Timothy 6:15

SHARE: What are some of the jobs and responsibilities of a king?

Because God is the great King over the whole earth, He is sovereign. That means He is in charge of everything, and everything ultimately belongs to Him. God is also completely good, so we can trust Him to always do what is right. He makes the rules because He knows what is best for us.

God, our King, has given us the Bible to help us know Him and to help us know what is right and what is wrong. He has given us boundaries so that we can freely live with Him in peace and security. When we disobey God's guidelines, we lose our peace, freedom, and security. But our King is so powerful that He can even make the bad things that happen when we do wrong things work together for the good of those who love Him (Romans 8:28).

While it is impossible to talk to the King of England or the President of the United States without a personal invitation, we can approach God's throne with confidence. We can talk to the greatest and most powerful King in the universe whenever we want to because Jesus, through His death and resurrection, has made a way for us to have direct access to God. And when we come to Him in prayer, He promises we will receive His loving kindness and all the help that we need (Hebrews 4:16).

Remember: if you believe in Jesus, you are a child of the highest King, and there is nothing too big or too small to talk to Him about. He has placed His hand of blessing on your head (Psalm 139:5).

PRAYER: *God, You are the great King over the whole earth. Thank You for wanting to spend time with me. Jesus, thank You for making that possible through Your death and resurrection. Help me want to spend more time with You.*

SHARE: What would you do if you were a king for a day?

GOD IS LOVE

"So we know that God loves us. We depend on it. God is love. Anyone who leads a life of love is joined to God. And God is joined to them."
– 1 John 4:16

SHARE: Do you feel most loved when someone gives you a hug, helps you with your chores, says some encouraging words to you, gives you a gift, or spends time with you?

God loves you deeply, even sacrificially. "God loved the world so much that He gave His one and only Son…" (John 3:16). God loves you more than anyone else ever can or will. And nothing can separate you from His love (Romans 8:38-39).

But that's not all. God **IS** love. And because God is love, He hates evil and injustice. God is patient, compassionate, forgiving, and kind. He is not rude or selfish or prideful. He is never grumpy or irritable. God always sees our potential and never gives up on us. His love for us never fails, no matter what we do or say or think (1 Corinthians 13:4-8). Because God loves us so much, He will also correct us when we are wrong to help us get back on the right track (Hebrews 12:6).

And God wants you to love Him too, with all your heart, with all your soul, and with all your mind (Matthew 22:37-38). Taking time to be with God is one way you can show your love to Him. He promises that when you draw near to Him, He will draw near to you (James 4:8). God not only loves you, He likes you, and He likes spending time with you.

Another way to show God our love for Him is to love other people (Matthew 22:39-40). But loving other people can be hard sometimes. Especially when they are unkind, and we don't think they deserve our love. "But here is how God has shown his love for us. While we were still sinners, Christ died for us" (Romans 5:8). We did nothing to deserve or earn God's love for us and yet He loves us anyway.

When we need help loving others well, we can always remember God's love for us and ask Him to fill us with His perfect, undeserved, never-ending, sacrificial love for them (Romans 5:5). When He pours His love into us, we can pour it out onto others (1 John 4:19).

PRAYER: *God, thank You for loving me like no one else can. Teach me how to love You with all my heart, soul, mind, and strength. And please show me how to share Your love with others (Luke 10:27).*

SHARE: What are some ways you can love God and others today?

GOD IS A MIRACLE WORKER

"You are the God who does miracles. You show your power among the nations." – Psalm 77:14

SHARE: What miracles have you witnessed or heard about?

A miracle is God's power on display in unexpected and often unexplainable ways. From the Bible we know that God parted the water so the Israelites could walk across safely on dry ground. God made a donkey talk (Numbers 22:28) and sent His angel to shut the mouths of the lions (Daniel 6:22). Jesus fed thousands of people with just five loaves of bread and two fish. He healed the sick, made the blind see, the deaf hear, the lame walk, and He brought the dead back to life.

Today, God STILL loves to use miracles to reveal Himself to us so that we can know Him better. But, sometimes we don't even notice God's miracles at all but explain them away as merely "good luck" or "science." And sometimes we are so focused on the miracles we are asking God to do for us that we miss the greater miracles God is doing in us, through us, and all around us.

Remember all the prayers He has answered in the past in your life and in others' lives. And keep praying those prayers that may seem impossible. Because with God, all things are possible (Matthew 19:26).

Sometimes miracles happen instantly. But, more often than not, they seem to come in slow motion and we have to wait.

As you wait for His answer, God may give you a fresh understanding of who He is and a new vision of His awesome plan for your life. God's plan is always better than we can ask or even imagine (Ephesians 3:20)! The greatest miracle is always God's presence with us.

PRAYER: *God, Your greatest miracle is that You brought Jesus back to life to overcome the power of sin and death. Thank You. Open my eyes to the miracles You are doing in me, through me, and around me so that I can know You better and so that I can help other people come to know You too.*

SHARE: What miracle would you like to ask God for?

GOD IS NEAR

"So let us come near to God with a sincere heart. Let us come near boldly because of our faith. Our hearts have been sprinkled. Our minds have been cleansed from a sense of guilt. Our bodies have been washed with pure water." – Hebrews 10:22

"But You are near, O LORD, and all your commands are true."
– Psalm 119:151 (NLT)

SHARE: When do you feel closest to God?

When you draw near to God, He promises to draw near to you (James 4:8).

You can draw near to God in all kinds of ways: through prayer, worship, reading your Bible, or being with other people who love Jesus, just to name a few. God longs for His children to be close to Him.

"(God) takes care of His flock like a shepherd. He gathers the lambs in his arms. He carries them close to his heart. He gently leads those that have little ones" (Isaiah 40:11). He is especially close to the brokenhearted, and He saves those who are crushed in spirit (Psalm 34:18). God is so close, His Spirit lives deep inside of everyone who believes and trusts in Jesus.

Sometimes we do wrong things that can make us feel like God is far away. He doesn't go anywhere. In fact, He promises to never leave us or forsake us (Hebrews 13:5). But our sin can block our awareness of His presence and make us feel distant from God.

When that happens, all we have to do is turn away from the wrong things we have done, turn toward God, and ask Him to forgive us—which He loves to do! "God is faithful and fair. If we admit that we have sinned, He will forgive us our sins. He will forgive every wrong thing we have done. He will make us pure" (1 John 1:9).

Remember, God is near. He will comfort you, forgive you, cleanse you, and help you whenever you turn to Him.

PRAYER: *Thank You, God, for Your Holy Spirit, who lives in me. Even when I can't see You or feel You, You are right here with me. Thank You that You promise to never leave me or forsake me. Show me if there is anything in my heart that makes You sad. Forgive me and make me pure.*

SHARE: Is there any sin you need to admit to God and ask Him to forgive? Talk to Him about it.

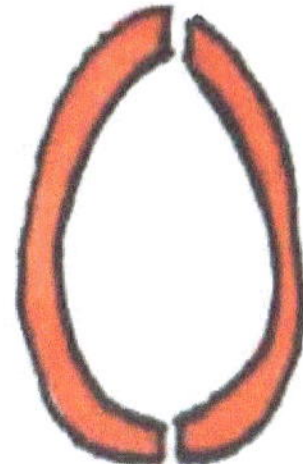# GOD IS OTHER

"I am God. There is no one like me." – Isaiah 46:9d

SHARE: How is God different from people?

God is completely other, totally different, unique, set apart from all created things. Another word for this is holy. He is sinless—perfectly pure and blameless. God is all-powerful, all-knowing, and present everywhere at the same time. There is no one like Him, nor has there ever been anyone like Him. Nothing in heaven or on earth can compare to Him. He alone is worthy of our worship. That is why the angels in heaven never stop singing,

> "'Holy, holy, holy
> is the Lord God who rules over all.'
> He was, and he is, and he will come." – Revelation 4:8d

God has called us to be holy too (1 Peter 1:16). Even though that seems impossible, we are God's children, and He wants us to talk and think and love like Him. He wants us to be different from people who do not know Him.

When we accept Jesus as our Savior and Lord, God takes away our sins and gives us Jesus' goodness. Then God sees **US** as holy. He sets us apart and makes us "other." Can you believe it?

And when we spend time with God, getting to know Him through His Word, talking with Him, listening to Him, and following Him, we become more and more "other," like Jesus.

PRAYER*: God, You are holy, and there is no one like You. You alone are worthy of my worship. Help me want to spend more time with You so that I can be more like Jesus. Please give me the courage to be different. Help me to do what is right in Your eyes, not the world's eyes, so that people know that I belong to You.*

SHARE: What can you do today to be less like the world and more like Jesus?

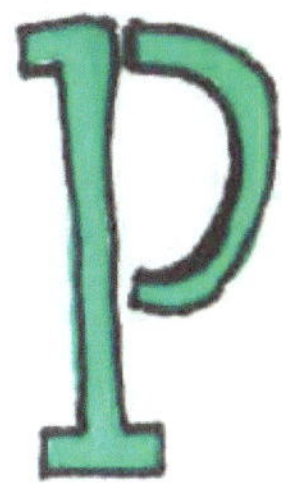

GOD IS THE POTTER

*"**LORD**, you are our Father. We are the clay. You are the potter. Your hands made all of us." – Isaiah 64:8*

SHARE: What have you made with your own hands?

Did you know that God is an artist, and we are His masterpieces?

God created us with great skill, care, and intention. How He made us is amazing and wonderful (Psalm 139:13-16). He shaped us and formed us in our mothers' bodies in His own image (Genesis 1:27). We were loved and known before we even took our first breath.

God created us on purpose for a purpose. His purpose for us is to be in His family and to do the good things that He prepared long ago for us to do (Ephesians 2:10). And He wants us to go and share His love with others so that they can come to know Him and the purpose for which He created them (Matthew 28:19-20).

God is personally involved in the everyday molding and shaping of our lives. Just like a potter shapes and reshapes wet clay into whatever form seems good to him, God uses our life circumstances (the good and the bad) to mold us and make us more beautiful … more like Jesus (Romans 8:28). His loving, gentle hands never leave us.

Because God created us, there is nothing beyond His power to fix, heal, or restore. We are extremely valuable, even priceless, because we are deeply loved by the masterful Artist who created us in His own image, and we belong to Him.

PRAYER: *God, You are the potter, and I am the clay. Your hands made me in Your own image. I am Your masterpiece, created to do the good things that You prepared long ago for me to do. Help me to trust that when life gets hard, You are reshaping me to make me even more beautiful—more like Jesus.*

SHARE: What are three things you like about the way God made you?

GOD IS QUIET

"… As the LORD approached, a very powerful wind tore the mountains apart. It broke up the rocks. But the LORD wasn't in the wind. After the wind there was an earthquake. But the LORD wasn't in the earthquake. After the earthquake a fire came. But the LORD wasn't in the fire. And after the fire there was only a gentle whisper." – 1 Kings 19:11-12

SHARE: When do you prefer quiet? When do you prefer noise?

God created us to know Him, not just know about Him. He created us to love Him and live our lives in the closest of friendships with Him. God wants us to talk to Him, and He wants to talk with us. Jesus says that we are His sheep, and His sheep listen to His voice (John 10:3). We can hear God's gentle whisper when we read the Bible and a word or phrase stands out to us. We can hear God speak through other believers like our pastor or our parents. Some people hear God speak to them through dreams. Sometimes He speaks to us through His Holy Spirit in our own thoughts and feelings and ideas. God is always speaking.

But God's voice is often quiet, so we need to move away from the distractions, noise, and chaos of our lives to hear Him. Phones, video games, a busy schedule, fear, doubt, worry, or anything that occupies too much of your time can prevent us from hearing God's gentle whispers. When was the last time you just sat quietly, read your Bible, and listened to God?

When we read God's Word, we get to know His personality, His character, the kinds of things He says and doesn't say. The more time we spend with Him in His Word, the better listeners we become, and we can more easily recognize when our own thoughts and activities have gotten out of line with God's character and personality. How amazing is it that we have access to words that are straight from God's very own mouth? It can take time to recognize when it is Him speaking, but hearing God is something we can learn how to do—something God wants us to learn so that we can grow closer to Him and become more like Him.

PRAYER: *God, please teach me to hear Your gentle, quiet whisper. Remind me every day to turn off the distractions, to sit quietly before You, to read Your Word, and to pay attention to what You are saying to me. And please give me the courage to do what You say.*

SHARE: What is the best time of day for you to spend some quiet time listening to God? Spend a few minutes quietly listening to God now. Is there a word or phrase that God is whispering to you from today's Bible verses?

GOD IS MY ROCK

"I love you, LORD. You give me strength. The LORD is my rock and my place of safety. He is the God who saves me. My God is my rock. I go to him for safety. He is like a shield to me. He's the power that saves me. He's my place of safety." – Psalm 18:1-2

SHARE: What do you do when you are afraid?

Some rocks are small and smooth, perfect for skipping on a lake, while others are HUGE—big enough to climb on and explore. God is solid and strong—like a big rock. He is a safe place to which we can always run.

How do we run to God? We can tell Him whenever we are scared, sad, or angry. When we talk with God about how we feel and trust that He sees us and hears us and loves us, He promises that He will be like a rock, shielding us and protecting us during life's storms.

Jesus once told His friends, "…everyone who hears my words and puts them into practice is like a wise man. He builds his house on the rock. The rain comes down. The water rises. The winds blow and beat against that house. But it does not fall. It is built on the rock" (Matthew 7:24-25).

When you build your life on God, making Him your most important thing by loving Him, serving Him, doing what He says, and trusting His promises in the Bible, then your life will be solid and unshakeable. Even when storms hit, God promises to hold you up, strengthen, and encourage you.

But making anything else the most important thing in your life—like money or friends or popularity or sports or school—is like building your life on unstable sand and will cause you to be overwhelmed and overcome when the storms of life hit.

When we build our lives on God, He promises to even use the storms, the hard things we go through in our lives, to make us strong and courageous (Isaiah 41:10). No matter what our circumstances are, we can always trust God to be there with us, helping us, and holding us tight (Psalm 139:10). He is faithful, trustworthy, everlasting, strong, immovable, and unshakeable … like a rock. And He is way more powerful than any storm!

PRAYER: *I love You, God. Help me to build my life on You. Help me to love You and trust You and do what You say. Remind me to run to You when I am sad, angry, or scared. Protect me and give me strength and courage when I need it. Hold me tight and help me hold tight to You.*

SHARE: What difficult thing are you (or someone you know) going through right now? Tell God how you feel and ask Him to help.

GOD IS MY SAVIOR

"God so loved the world that he gave his one and only Son. Anyone who believes in him will not die but will have eternal life. God did not send his Son into the world to judge the world. He sent his Son to save the world through him." – John 3:16-17

SHARE: Talk about a time when you disobeyed. What were the consequences?

When God created the world and everything in it, He said it was very good. But Adam and Eve, the people He so lovingly created, disobeyed God in the Garden of Eden. Their sin corrupted God's good design, and their relationship with their heavenly Father was broken.

The Bible tells us that we all inherited a sinful nature from Adam and Eve that separates us from God too (Romans 3:23). You see, God is holy and fair, and He cannot let disobedience and rebellion go unpunished. Death is the consequence of our sin (Romans 6:23) so that we don't live forever in our sinfulness (Genesis 3:22).

But here is the Good News! Because our heavenly Father loves us with all His heart and wants to be with us and live with us forever, He sent His only Son Jesus to save us. Jesus died on a cross in our place for our sins (John 3:16-17). He willingly took our sin on Himself so that we could be clean, forgiven, and free.

And here is more good news! God miraculously brought Jesus back to life on the third day after He died. He conquered sin and death so that we could live with Him forever. Jesus is now alive in heaven with the Father praying for us and preparing a home for us (John 14:3). God has sent His Holy Spirit to live in us until the day Jesus comes back again to rule as King of heaven and earth. Everyone who loves, follows, and believes in Jesus will live with Him for all eternity.

God wants you to accept Jesus' forgiveness for your sins so that you can live forever with Him. It is as simple as ABC …

>   A – **ADMIT** to God that you have disobeyed Him and ask Him to forgive you.
>   B – **BELIEVE** that God sent His Son Jesus to die on a cross for your sins.
>   C – **CHOOSE** to follow Jesus and let Him be in charge of your life.

PRAYER*: God, I **admit** that I have disobeyed You. Please forgive me. I **believe** You love me so much that You sent Your Son Jesus to die for my sins. Thank You. I know Jesus is alive and has sent His Holy Spirit to live in me, so I **choose** to follow You, Jesus, wherever You lead. Thank You, God, for saving me and for making me clean and new and a part of Your family forever!*

SHARE: When did you first come to know Jesus as your Savior? As soon as New Testament Christians confessed their belief in Jesus, they were baptized to show others that they were now a part of God's family (see Acts 8:26-39). Have you been baptized?

GOD IS THREE-IN-ONE

"As soon as Jesus was baptized, he came up out of the water. At that moment heaven was opened. Jesus saw the Spirit of God coming down on him like a dove. A voice from heaven said, "This is my Son, and I love him. I am very pleased with him." – Matthew 3:16-17

"How good and pleasant it is when God's people live together in peace!" – Psalm 133:1

SHARE: What would the perfect family be like?

The fancy word for three-in-one is trinity. Our God exists in three distinct persons: God the Father, Jesus the Son, and the Holy Spirit. But they are all one God.

OUR HEAVENLY FATHER IS GOD: seated in heaven on His throne, ruling and reigning over this world with love and justice, forgiving us, providing for us, strengthening us, protecting us, and making all things new (Philippians 4:19; Revelation 4:2-3; 21:5).

JESUS THE SON IS GOD: after living, suffering, dying, and rising again, He is now seated at the right hand of the Father praying for us, loving us, speaking to our hearts, preparing a place for us, and planning for His return (John 1:1; 14:2-3; Romans 8:34).

THE HOLY SPIRIT IS GOD: living inside of every follower of Jesus, helping us, guiding us, leading us, praying for us, revealing Truth to us, and pouring out the Father's love into our hearts (John 14:16-17; 16:13; Romans 5:5; 8:26).

They are one God in three persons, in perfect community, working together to show us who God is and what He is like. God made us to be in community too—in close relationship with Him and with other people. It is not good for us to be alone (Genesis 2:18) because God has created us to be like Him in healthy, loving relationships.

Relationships can be hard for us sometimes because we are all selfish and prideful, and sometimes our feelings get hurt. But God desires for us to live together in perfect, unbroken relationship with Him and with others as one big, happy family. Working together to love and forgive each other in our friendships and families is important to God so that we look more like Him. But we cannot do it in our own strength. We need God's help to do this well.

PRAYER: *God, thank You for loving me and making me a part of Your family. Thank You for my family. Help us to forgive each other and love each other well. Also, please help me make good friends and help me be a good friend too.*

SHARE: Is there a relationship you would like God to help you with? Talk to Him about it.

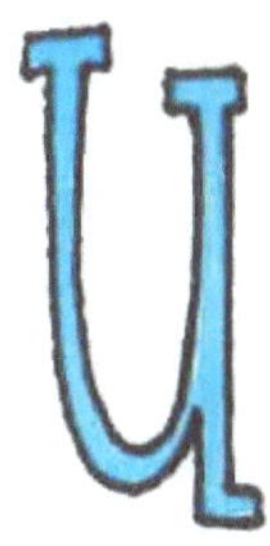

GOD IS UNCHANGING

"I am the LORD. I do not change..." – Malachi 3:6

"Jesus Christ is the same yesterday and today and forever."
– Hebrews 13:8

SHARE: What things in your life have changed recently?

It seems like everything in this world changes. Our feelings and moods change depending on how hungry or tired we are. Caterpillars transform into butterflies. Green leaves turn yellow, orange, and red in the fall. Our interests, teachers, and friends all change as we grow.

But God never changes.

> When you feel lonely … God is always with you.
> When you feel weak … God is always strong.
> When you feel scared or anxious or nervous or mad … God is always your peace.
> When you feel sad … God will always comfort you.
> When God doesn't answer your prayer the way you want Him to … He is still good.
> When you can't seem to hear or see Him … God is still real.
> When your plans are not God's plans … He always has something better for you.
> When the world seems out of control … God is always on His throne, and nothing surprises Him.
> No matter what you do, say, or think … God will never stop loving you.

Because God's love never changes. God is the same today as He was in Bible times, and He will be the same forever. Throughout history He has been good, powerful, faithful, and loving. He will always be kind and compassionate. And He will never leave us or forsake us (Deuteronomy 31:8, Hebrews 13:5).

PRAYER: *God, in this world that is constantly changing, it is comforting to know that You remain the same forever. You will always be faithful and kind and good. You will always love and forgive me. I can trust You. Help me to be trustworthy too.*

SHARE: Do you like change? Why or why not?

GOD IS VICTORIOUS

"So do not be afraid. I am with you. Do not be terrified. I am your God. I will make you strong and help you. I will hold you safe in my hands. I always do what is right." – Isaiah 41:10

"But let us give thanks to God! He gives us the victory because of what our Lord Jesus Christ has done." – 1 Corinthians 15:57

SHARE: Who is your favorite superhero? Why?

Every superhero movie has a good character and a bad character. We always root for the good ones, and in the end, they usually win.

In real life, when we hear about sad things happening around the world, it may seem like the bad people are winning. But the Bible tells us that in the end, good conquers evil in real life too, because God is the ultimate superhero. He is all-powerful, all-knowing, all-seeing, and all-loving. With God, nothing is impossible (Luke 1:37).

Jesus defeated evil by dying on the cross and rising from the dead.

Today, God uses us to help others and to spread His goodness and love around the world.

And one day soon, "The God who gives peace will soon crush Satan under your feet" (Romans 16:20a) and destroy evil completely. Jesus will return to reign victoriously as King, and there will be no more suffering, sin, or sadness. Good will triumph over evil.

We know how this real-life story ends—our God is victorious!

PRAYER: *Thank You, God, that You have already won the battle of good and evil through Jesus. I am so glad that I am on Your side and that You are on my side! As I wait for You, help me to help others and spread Your goodness and love everywhere I go.*

SHARE: What are you looking forward to the most when Jesus returns?

Eternal Life
ONE WAY

GOD IS WELCOMING

"Jesus said, 'Let the little children come to me. Don't keep them away. The kingdom of heaven belongs to people like them.'" – Matthew 19:14

"The Lord is not slow to keep his promise. He is not slow in the way some people understand it. Instead, he is patient with you. He doesn't want anyone to be destroyed. Instead, he wants all people to turn away from their sins." – 2 Peter 3:9

SHARE: If you could invite anyone to dinner (from the past or the present), who would it be?

God loves everyone in the whole world (John 3:16)—no matter how old you are or how much money you have or where you live. He wants all of us to know Him and love Him and be with Him forever.

God made one way for us to know Him. That way is Jesus. Jesus said, "I am <u>the</u> way and <u>the</u> truth and <u>the</u> life. No one comes to the Father except through me" (John 14:6, emphasis added).

Not everyone chooses to believe in and follow Jesus. Some want Jesus to be a way, but not the only way. Some choose to go their own way, so not everyone gets to live with God forever. Jesus is the only way to have a relationship with God the Father.

God says, "Come, all you who are thirsty. Come and drink the water I offer to you. You who do not have any money, come. Buy and eat the grain I give you. Come and buy wine and milk. You will not have to pay anything for it. Why spend money on what is not food? Why work for what does not satisfy you? Listen carefully to me. Then you will eat what is good. You will enjoy the richest food there is. Listen and come to me. Pay attention to me. Then you will live. I will make a covenant with you that will last forever. I will give you my faithful love ..." (Isaiah 55:1-3).

God is not actually talking about food and drinks here. He is inviting each one of us into a growing, loving, joy-filled relationship with Him. Do you want that too?

God loves everyone, and He shows His mercy and kindness to all (Matthew 5:45). He welcomes all people into His family, but we must accept His invitation (Luke 14:15-24) and come to Him His way—through faith in Jesus.

PRAYER: *Thank You, God, for inviting and welcoming me into Your family. I accept Your invitation! Show me who I can be welcoming to today.*

SHARE: Who would you like to invite and help welcome into God's family? Talk to God about it.

GOD IS THE X-FACTOR

"I know what it's like not to have what I need. I also know what it's like to have more than I need. I have learned the secret of being content no matter what happens. I am content whether I am well fed or hungry. I am content whether I have more than enough or not enough. I can do all this by the power of Christ. He gives me strength." – Philippians 4:12-13

SHARE: If you could have any superpower, what would it be?

An X-factor is an indescribable quality, a difference maker, a game changer, a strong but unpredictable influence.

God is our difference maker. He is our secret ingredient, our secret sauce. He does things that no one sees coming.

> Moses parted the Red Sea … with God.
> The walls of Jericho came crashing down … with God.
> Gideon conquered enemy armies … with God.
> David defeated Goliath … with God.
> Elijah called fire down from heaven … with God.
> Daniel survived a den of lions … with God.
> Esther saved her people … with God.
> The disciples healed people, drove out demons, and spoke in languages they didn't know … with God.
> Paul was content even when he suffered … with God.

God makes the difference in everything we do. He gives us power, strength, wisdom, anything we need to do whatever He asks us to do.

Nothing is impossible … with God.

PRAYER: *God, I can do everything you ask me to do by Your power. You give me strength. You are my secret sauce. You make all the difference in my life. Show me what You want me to do today … with You. And may I give You all the glory!*

SHARE: What do you dream of doing … with God?

Hello
my name is

GOD IS YAHWEH

"God said to Moses, 'I AM WHO I AM. Here is what you must say to the Israelites. Tell them, "I AM has sent me to you." … 'My name will always be The LORD (Yahweh). Call me this name for all time to come.'"
— Exodus 3:14-15

SHARE: If you could choose your own name, what would it be?

Names are important. Your parents chose your name lovingly and purposefully. They either knew someone they admired with your name, or it has a special meaning, or they simply loved the way it sounded. God knows your name (Isaiah 43:1), but have you ever wondered what His name is?

When Moses was first getting to know God, he asked God what he should call Him. God answered, "Yahweh" (often translated in English Bibles as *"The LORD"*). Yahweh is a word in the Hebrew language that means "I am" or "the one who is." This suggests that God is eternal and uncreated. He was, He is, and He forever will be.

Jesus is the visible image of the invisible Yahweh (Colossians 1:15). And Jesus used *"I AM"* to describe Himself many times:

> *I AM* the bread of life (John 6:35),
> *I AM* the light of the world. (John 8:12),
> *I AM* the door (John 10:7),
> *I AM* the good shepherd (John 10:11, 14),
> *I AM* the resurrection and the life (John 11:25),
> *I AM* the way, the truth, and the life (John 14:6), and
> *I AM* the true vine (John 15:1).

He also said, "What I'm about to tell you is true. … Before Abraham was born, *I AM*!" (John 8:58, emphasis added). But many people refused to believe Jesus, so they never got to know Him.

Do you want to know Him? Knowing God starts with knowing His name. God wanted Moses to know Him so that God could do amazing things in and through him.

Jesus wants us to know Him too, so that we can become part of God's family (John 1:12), and so that He can do amazing things in, through, and with us forever.

PRAYER: *God, You are the eternal, uncreated God who is and who was and who always will be. Thank You for making a way for me to know You through Your Word and through Your Holy Spirit living in me.*

SHARE: How did your parents choose your name? What does your name mean?

THERE ARE A ZILLION MORE THINGS TO LEARN ABOUT GOD

"Jesus also did many other things. What if every one of them were written down? I suppose that even the whole world would not have room for the books that would be written." – John 21:25

SHARE: What is the biggest number you can name? (Infinity doesn't count—it's not an actual number!)

A zillion sounds like an actual number because of its similarity to billion, million, and trillion. But, like infinity, zillion is just a general way to talk about a very large number that goes on forever—like how many grains of sand are on the seashore or the number of stars in the sky.

God goes on forever and ever too. He has no beginning and no end. Because He is eternal, we will never know everything about Him, but we get to spend our whole lives and all of eternity with Him getting to know Him better.

God wants us to know Him—inside and out, beginning to end, from A to Z. And then He wants us to keep on knowing Him more every day. That is why He gave us His creation. That is why He gave us His very own words in the Bible. That is why He gave us His Spirit. That is why He gave us the Church.

The more we know God, the stronger we grow in Him, and the better we know ourselves and who He created us to be. He longs for a deeper relationship with us. He wants to talk with us. He wants us to enjoy spending time with Him. He wants to have conversations with us and laugh and cry with us. He wants us to get to know Him—really know Him personally—not just believe in Him. And as you get to know Him better, you will discover other characteristics of God and grow in your relationship with Him.

PRAYER: *God, please help me to make it a priority to read my Bible every day so that I can get to know You better. Help me to see You and hear You all throughout my day so that I can experience for myself Your love and forgiveness.*

SHARE: You did it…you made it to the letter Z! This book is not a complete list of God's amazing qualities—that book would be a zillion pages long. Which other words can you think of to describe God from A to Z?

ACKNOWLEDGMENTS

Thank you to Steve, first and foremost. This book would not even exist without your creative genius. I loved brainstorming ideas with you on our summer evening walks. Thank you for your patient diligence as the first editor. And thank you for being my biggest encourager.

Thank you to Kelly for your whimsical illustrations. They make the whole book! Your artistic style always makes me smile.

Thank you to Kristi Knowles for your publishing expertise and for pulling everything together.

Thank you to Rachel White (and family), Julie Hawkins, and Holly Wilcox (my favorite sister) for the time you took out of your busy schedules and families to help me through this first book. Your thoughtful feedback has made it so much better.

Special thanks to Dr. Gregory Hall (*RethinkingScripture.com*) for your thorough revisions and theological acumen. (You have clearly found your thing to do and your place to be!) I am grateful for your wisdom, experience, expertise, kind patience, and timely responses to my many questions. I learned so much from you.

And finally, thank You, God. This is from You and for You. Please use it to help others come to know You.

RESOURCES THAT HAVE ENCOURAGED ME ON MY PARENTING JOURNEY:

MomsInPrayer.org,
BibleProject.com,
ChristianParenting.com,
Lectio for Families (a free devotional app),
Foundation Worldview Podcast,
Raising Boys and Girls Podcast

ABOUT THE AUTHOR:

Kim is an avid reader and lifelong Northwesterner. A former teacher, she has a master's degree in elementary education. After teaching full-time and then raising twins, Kim now substitute teaches, volunteers with youth at her church, and leads a prayer ministry for moms with school-aged children through Moms in Prayer International. Kim and her husband Steve have two grown children and live in Gig Harbor, Washington. Kim's passion is to impact the next generation by helping children and families grow closer to God through Bible study and prayer. You can follow Kim on Instagram @WhoIsGodBook *or* contact her through her website at WhoIsGodFromAtoZ.com.

Kim (R) and Kelly (L) have lived across the street from each other
for nearly 14 years. This book is their first project together.

ABOUT THE ILLUSTRATOR:

Kelly has always been passionate about creating and doing artwork. Her creative interest led to a Bachelor of Arts degree in design. After graduating from Washington State University, she worked in Interior Design and as a freelance artist creating illustrations, carvings, and paintings. She has also written and illustrated the whimsical children's book Beatrice the Bee and its companion coloring book Color Me Beatrice the Bee. Kelly and her husband Peter have two grown children and live in Gig Harbor, Washington with their two dogs. You can follow Kelly on Instagram @KellyJohnsonArt and at www.etsy.com/shop/KDJART or contact her at KellyJohnsonChildrensBooks@gmail.com.

PRAYER SQUARES

PARENTS, CUT OUT EACH SQUARE AND USE AS A DAILY PROMPT TO PRAY FOR YOUR CHILDREN.	**A** MAY THEY KNOW AND BELIEVE THAT YOU ARE ABSOLUTELY TRUE.	**B** OPEN THEIR EYES TO YOUR BEAUTY AND GIVE THEM GRATEFUL HEARTS.

C MAY THEY GIVE ALL THEIR WORRIES TO YOU BECAUSE YOU CARE FOR THEM.	**D** DEFEND THEM, LORD. FIGHT FOR THEM TODAY.	**E** MAY THEY KNOW HOW MUCH YOU LOVE THEM. PLANT THEM DEEPLY IN YOUR LOVE.	**F** HELP THEM TO TRUST YOU TO DO WHAT IS BEST.
G MAY THEY NOT GROW WEARY IN DOING GOOD.	**H** MAY THEY PRAY CONTINUOUSLY AND NEVER STOP.	**I** HELP THEM TO SEE YOU, OTHERS, AND THEMSELVES AS YOU DO.	**J** FILL THEM WITH JOY, EVEN ON HARD DAYS.
K MAY THEY APPROACH YOUR THRONE OF GRACE WITH CONFIDENCE.	**L** TEACH THEM TO LOVE YOU WITH ALL THEIR HEARTS, SOULS, MINDS, AND STRENGTH.	**M** WORK MIRACLES IN THEIR LIVES, LORD, AND HELP THEM TO RECOGNIZE THEM.	**N** HELP THEM TO RECOGNIZE THEIR SIN AND CONFESS IT TO YOU.
O GROW THEM MORE AND MORE LIKE JESUS.	**P** HELP THEM TO APPRECIATE HOW YOU CREATED THEM - ON PURPOSE FOR A PURPOSE.	**Q** HELP THEM TO HEAR YOU AND GIVE THEM THE COURAGE TO DO WHAT YOU SAY.	**R** HELP THEM TO BUILD THEIR LIVES ON YOU.
S SAVE THEM, GOD! MAY THEY KNOW JESUS AS THEIR SAVIOR AND LORD.	**T** GIVE THEM STRONG, HEALTHY RELATIONSHIPS WITH FAMILY AND FRIENDS.	**U** HELP THEM TO BE HONEST AND TRUSTWORTHY LIKE YOU.	**V** DELIVER THEM FROM THE EVIL ONE, FROM THIS WORLD, AND FROM SELFISH DESIRES.
W MAY THEY BE WELCOMING, COMPASSIONATE, AND KIND.	**X** MAY THEY BELIEVE ALL THINGS ARE POSSIBLE…WITH GOD!	**Y** INCREASE THEIR DESIRE TO KNOW YOU, GOD.	**Z** HELP THEM TO ENJOY READING THEIR BIBLES AND WORSHIPING YOU.

www.ingramcontent.com/pod-product-compliance
Lightning Source LLC
Chambersburg PA
CBHW042045110726
48006CB00002B/294